THE NEW ANDY CAPP COLLECTION

NUMBER 2

David and Charles

Edited by Duncan Ion

Cartoons: Roger Kettle & Roger Mahoney
Graphics: Richard Sunderland

Visit Andy at www.andycapp.com

A DAVID & CHARLES BOOK
David & Charles is a subsidiary of F+W (UK) Ltd.,
an F+W Publications Inc. company

First published in the UK in 2005

A catalogue record for this book is available from the British Library.

ISBN 0 7153 2165 X

Printed in Singapore by KHL Printing Co Pte Ltd.
for David & Charles
Brunel House   Newton Abbot   Devon

Visit our website at **www.davidandcharles.co.uk**

David & Charles books are available from all good bookshops;
alternatively you can contact our Orderline on 0870 9908222 or
write to us at FREEPOST EX2 110, D&C Direct, Newton Abbot,
TQ12 4ZZ (no stamp required UK mainland).

EMPLOYMENT AGENCY

I HAVE THE FORM YOU FILLED IN, MISTER CAPP

I WAS WONDERING IF THERE WERE ANY *OTHER* JOBS YOU MIGHT BE WILLING TO CONSIDER...

...APART FROM "*LAMP LIGHTER*" AND "*WHALE HUNTER*"?

I DIDN'T SEE YOU AT THE DOG RACING LAS'NIGHT, TOM—

I WENT TO THE PUB INSTEAD AND HAD A REAL NICE EVENING WITH MY MISSUS

THE WAY *MY* LUCK'S GOING, ONE OF THESE NIGHTS I CAN SEE THAT HAPPENING TO *ME!*

TRAVEL AGENT

THERE ARE SO MANY BARGAINS AT THE MOMENT

TRAVEL AGENT

THE PROBLEM IS FINDING ONE TO SUIT YOU

TRAVEL AGENT

LET'S SEE...SKIING... PARAGLIDING... WIND-SURFING... NOPE — NO SIGN OF INTENSIVE NAPPING

WHAT CAN I SAY THAT I HAVEN'T ALREADY SAID TO HIM? ALL I WANT IS TO GET MESELF T' BED...

GRRRR

I'M TERRIBLY SORRY, PET — I SWEAR I'LL BE EARLIER IN THE FUTURE

DON'T KNOW WHY I WASTE MY TIME — A DIRTY LOOK IS AS GOOD AS A SPEECH ANY DAY

WELL?

I GOT SENT OFF FOR THROWING THE REF'S WHISTLE AWAY

THAT SEEMS A BIT HARSH

IT WAS STILL IN HIS MOUTH AT THE TIME

BILLY'S WEDDING WENT WELL, GIVEN THE CIRCUMSTANCES

APART FROM THE AWKWARD MOMENT WHEN HE WENT TO PUT THE RING ON THE BRIDE'S FINGER ....

.... AND THE GUARD HAD TO UNLOCK HIS HANDCUFFS

VERY DISCREET, THOUGH

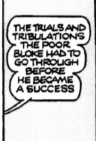

WHEN MOST PEOPLE COUNT TO TEN, THEY USE THE TIME TO CALM THEMSELVES DOWN

HE USES IT TO TAKE AIM

TCH! THE WAGES SOME OF THESE FOOTBALLERS GET— THREE MILLION A YEAR!

LET'S SEE — THAT WORKS OUT AT ABOUT ONE POINT FIVE MILLION A YEAR

HE CALCULATES SALARIES IN BEERS

FLO WON'T BE HOME FOR AGES — I'D BETTER GET MYSELF SOMETHING TO EAT

"EMPTY CONTENTS INTO A SAUCEPAN AND BRING TO A BOIL, STIRRING CONTINUOUSLY"

"STIRRING CONTINUOUSLY"?

FLO WILL BE HOME SOON

YOU CERTAINLY SURPRISED OUR OPPONENTS WITH THAT DEFENSIVE TACTIC OF YOURS

THEY'D NEVER SEEN ANYONE LIE ACROSS THE TABLE IN FRONT OF THE POCKETS BEFORE

WOULD YOU MIND DOING SOME SHOPPING FOR ME WHILE I'M AT WORK?

COULD YOU GET SOME MILK, SOME BREAD...

...AND SOMETHING TO CURE MY BLIND OPTIMISM?

AH, YES — THE KIND OF CURRENT AFFAIRS DEBATE YOU ONLY HEAR IN A MODERN, TRENDY ESTABLISHMENT...

...WAS PERRY COMO A BETTER SINGER THAN DEAN MARTIN?

PETER'S MOVED FROM BANKING TO ACCOUNTANCY

HE FELT IT WAS TIME FOR A CAREER CHANGE

ANDY DID THAT THIRTY YEARS AGO

HE MOVED FROM THE ARMCHAIR TO THE COUCH

SIGH

WHAT'S UP, VICAR?

CHURCH ATTENDANCE, ANDY— LAST NIGHT'S WAS THE LOWEST EVER

WHEN I SAID, "AMEN," IT ECHOED FOR TWENTY MINUTES

LOANS

NO, I'M AFRAID YOUR REPAYMENTS WOULD HAVE TO BE MADE IN CASH

LOANS

HAVING YOUR WIFE WASH OUR DISHES IS NOT AN OPTION

TCH! THE FASHIONS TODAY — LOOK AT THOSE SKIRTS!

I'VE USED MORE MATERIAL SEWING ON A NAME TAG

SO — YOUR HOUSE IS ON FIRE... WHAT DO YOU DO FIRST?

SAVE MY POOL CUE

AFTER, OF COURSE, MAKING SURE MY WIFE WAS ABSOLUTELY, POSITIVELY IN NO DANGER WHATSOEVER

WHAT A DAY — AM I GLAD TO BE HOME!

ANY POST FOR ME TODAY? PHONE CALLS?

WOULD YOU LIKE A BEER?

PLEASE

HIS BRAIN HAS DEVELOPED A FILTER SYSTEM — "BEER" IS ONE OF THE FEW WORDS THAT GETS THROUGH

SIGH...

OH, FOR GOODNESS' SAKE, TAKE SOME MONEY AND GO TO THE PUB!

WAIT A MINUTE! IS THIS OUT OF PITY?

BECAUSE IF IT IS — ACTUALLY, I DON'T HAVE A PROBLEM WITH THAT

MARRIAGE GUIDANCE

I JUST WISH HE WERE A BIT MORE ROMANTIC

I BROUGHT HOME SOME FLOWERS LAST NIGHT

THAT'S TRUE

HE FELL IN A ROSE BUSH, COMING BACK FROM THE PUB — THEY WERE STUCK TO HIS JACKET

THAT'S NOT THE POINT

I DOUBT IF I'LL MAKE THE PUB TONIGHT, ANDY — I PROMISED RUBE I'D PAINT THE KITCHEN

WOULD SOME HELP SPEED THINGS UP?

DEFINITELY

OKAY — I'LL SEND FLO ROUND AND SEE YOU IN THE PUB LATER

NEW FACE, JACK, AND PRETTY WITH IT—

YOU'RE WASTING YOUR TIME, ANDY— SHE'S A SUNDAY SCHOOL TEACHER

OH, I DON'T KNOW, JACK, WITH LOOKS LIKE THAT, SHE CAN'T BE ALL GOOD

ARE YOU LISTENING? I SAID I'VE NEVER BEEN SO MISERABLE—

I'M LISTENING, BUT WHAT CAN I DO?

YOU COULD AT LEAST FEEL FOR ME!

NOT EVEN HALF A PINT, IF YOU DON'T BELIEVE ME, COME AND FEEL FOR YOURSELF

DID THE CARPENTER COME, PET?

YES, BUT HE WOULDN'T TACKLE THE JOB, SAID IT WAS NEXT TO IMPOSSIBLE

WHAT HAPPENS NOW?

YOU KNOW ME, PET, WHEN THEY SAY A THING CAN'T BE DONE

DEFINITELY—

DON'T BOTHER TO TRY

Printed in Great Britain
by Amazon